THE BOSS

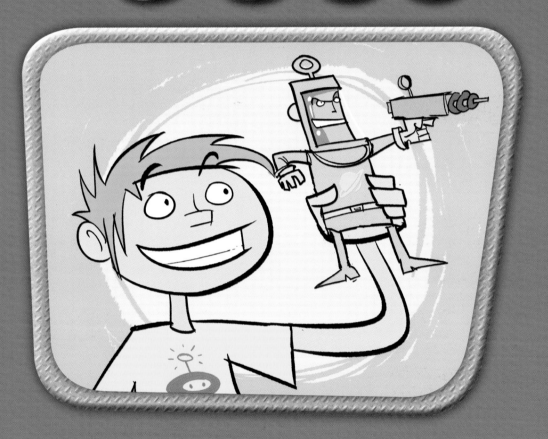

Written by Dale Tenby

Illustrated by Steve May

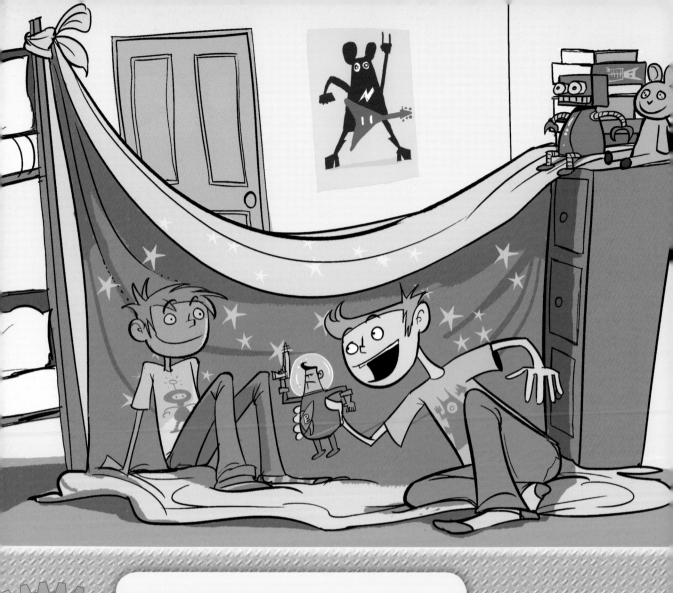

Dex was in Nick's den.

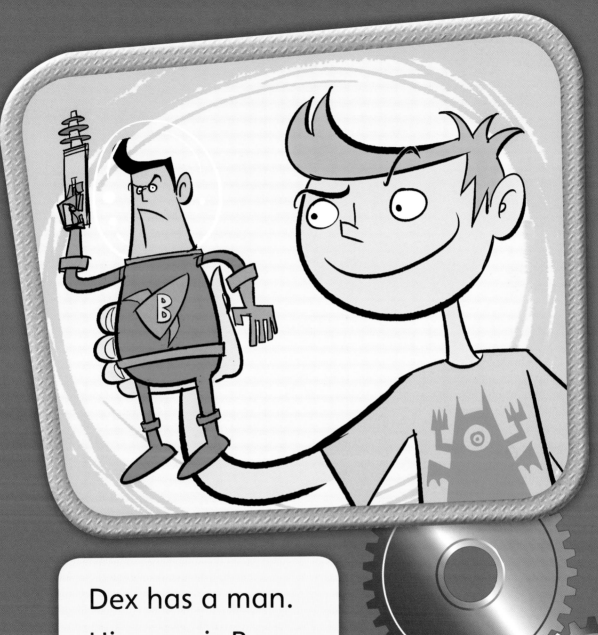

Dex has a man.

His man is Bazz.

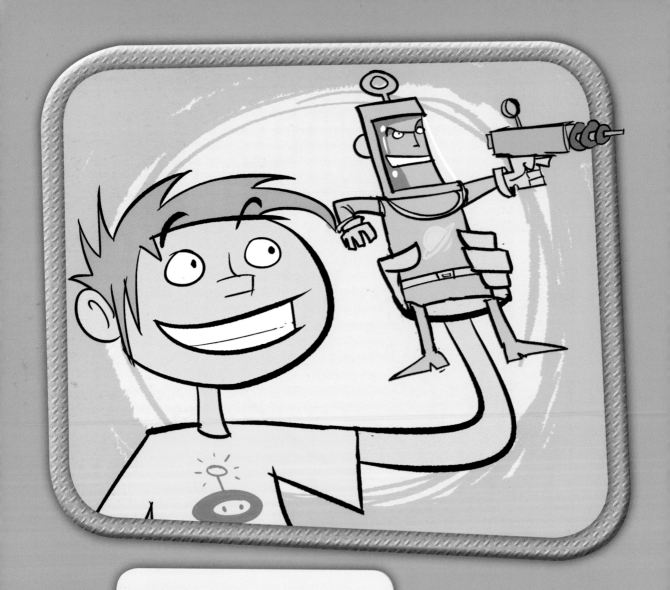

Nick has a man.
His man is Bill.

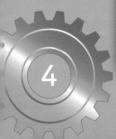

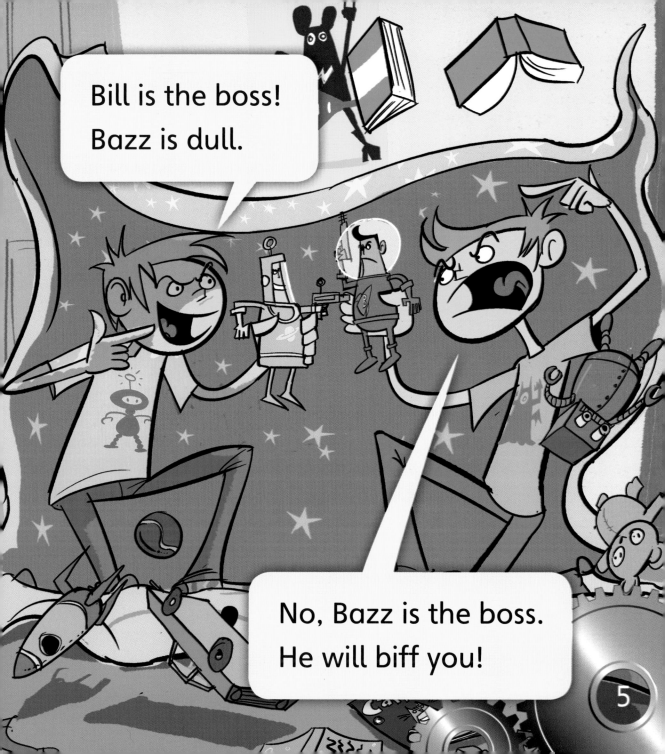

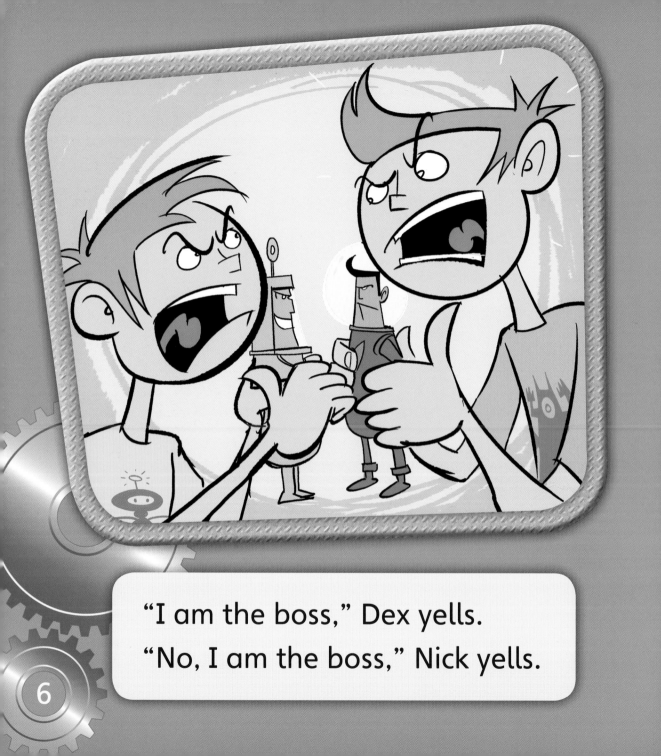

"I am the boss," Dex yells.

"No, I am the boss," Nick yells.

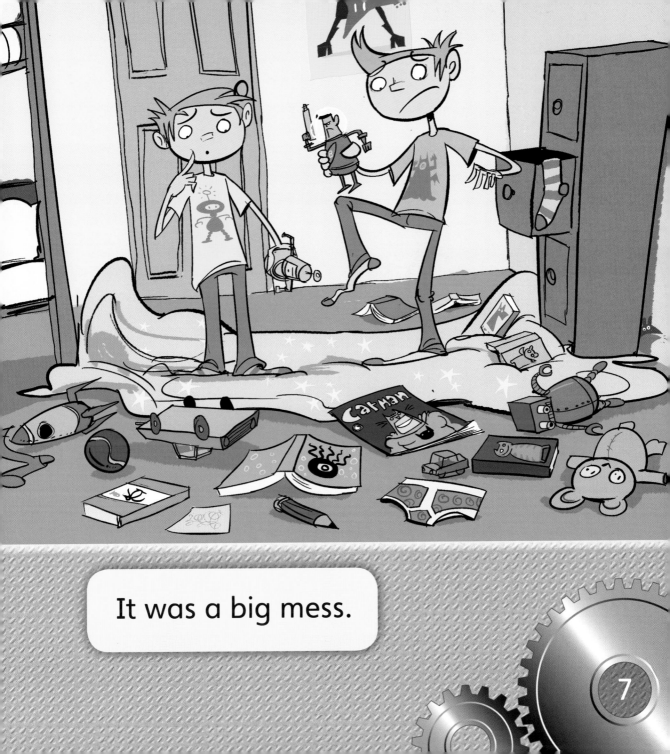

It was a big mess.

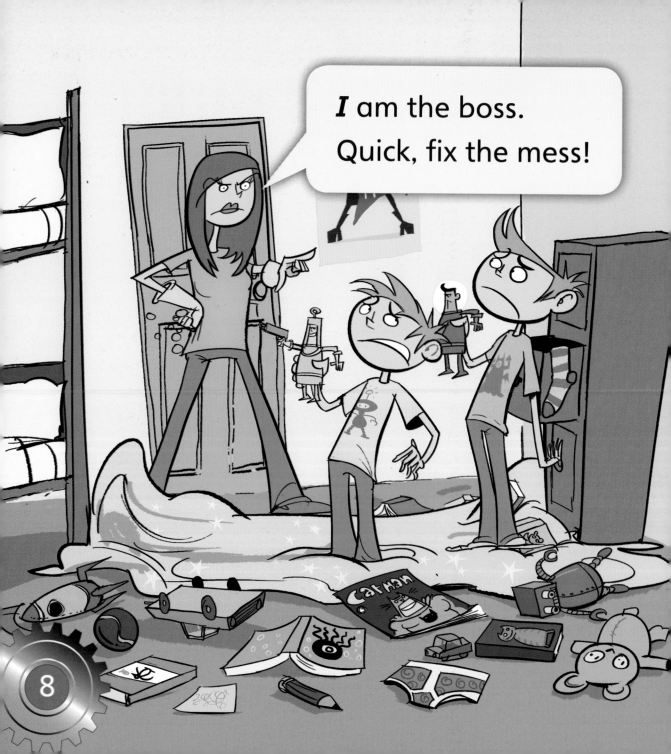